P

american popular piano

SKILLS

SKILLS

Created by
Dr. Scott
McBride Smith

T0056211

Series Composer
Christopher
Norton

Editor
Dr. Scott
McBride Smith

Associate Editor
Clarke
MacIntosh

SKILLS

SKILLS

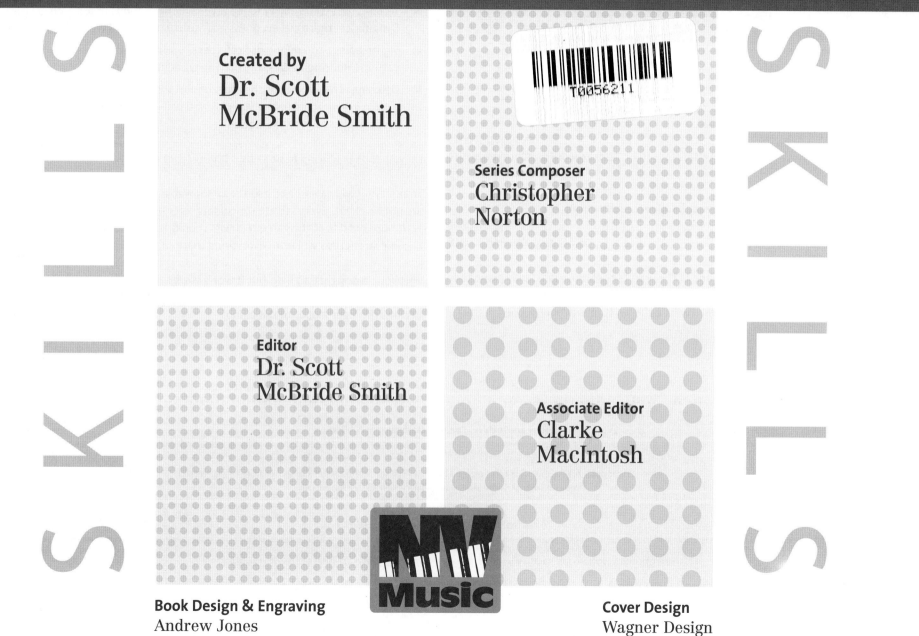

NV Music

Book Design & Engraving
Andrew Jones

Cover Design
Wagner Design

Introduction

Everyone agrees that Tiger Woods is one of the greatest golfers of all time. Some even think he is the best ever! He won the 1997 Masters Tournament when he was 21 years old, the youngest winner in history. He was also the youngest golfer to complete a career *Grand Slam*, winning all four major championships by the age of 25.
How did he do it? Let's see what he says.

From early childhood I dreamed of being the world's best golfer. I worked hard and applied my family's values to everything I did. Integrity, honesty, discipline, responsiblity and fun; I learned these values at home and in school, each one pushing me further toward my dream.

Eldrick (Tiger) Woods
Letter from Tiger, Tiger Woods Foundation Website
http://www.twfound.org

The best way to achieve [a] goal is through sound fundamentals.

Tiger Woods
Golf Digest, November 1998

What's your dream? Do you want to be one of the world's best musicians? play piano for your own enjoyment? or entertain your friends and family? No matter which, Tiger is right. Hard work, responsibility – and fun! – will be the keystones to your success.

In golf, the term "fundamentals" covers many things. In piano-playing, we can break it down into three broad groupings.

- **Technic.** This is the ability to readily make the motions that create beautiful sounds. Dynamic control, tonal evenness and variety, and speed would fall into this category.
- **Sightreading.** You might also call these "quick learning" skills. Seeing patterns, noticing details, and playing without stopping – right away.
- **Listening.** This is perhaps the most important of all! If you can't hear the sounds of a piece in your mind before you play, you will never do a good job performing it. Psychologists call this "audiation".

Do you think practicing basic skills is boring? Get over it!

Your playing will never be as good or as enjoyable as you want it to be if your basic skills are not excellent. Every athlete – including Tiger – spends time on drills, exercises and warm-ups outside of the game. Pianists should, too. When your piano fundamentals become strong, you will learn everything more easily and perform more confidently.

This book is designed to help, but it won't work if you don't! Practice carefully and frequently. Spend some time every day on your basic skills and, who knows ... you may become the Tiger Woods of the piano.

Library and Archives Canada Cataloguing in Publication

Smith, Scott McBride

American popular piano [music] : skills / created by Scott McBride Smith ; Series Composer, Christopher Norton ; editor, Scott McBride Smith ; associate editor, Clarke MacIntosh.

To be complete in 11 volumes.
Contents: Preparatory level -- Level 1 -- Level 2.
Miscellaneous information: The series is organized in 11 levels, from preparatory to level 10, each including a repertoire album, an etudes album, a skills book, and an instrumental backings compact disc.

ISBN 978-1-897379-22-6 (preparatory level).--ISBN 978-1-897379-23-3 (level 1).--ISBN 978-1-897379-24-0 (level 2)

1. Piano--Studies and exercises. 2. Piano--Studies and exercises--Juvenile. I. Norton, Christopher, 1953- II. MacIntosh, S. Clarke, 1959- III. Title.

MT225.S659 2007   786.2'142   C2007-905832-9

Table of Contents

Unit 1 - Module 1

A. Brainthumpers

Play these notes with the written fingering while counting out loud.
Practice daily.

1) 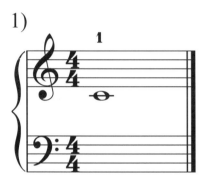   2)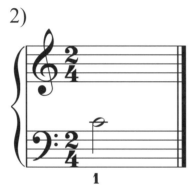

B. Technic

Practice daily, hands separate (S) or together (T).

1) Pentascales (pages 42-43)

No. ____ ; key _____ ; M.M. _____ ; S / T

No. ____ ; key _____ ; M.M. _____ ; S / T

2) Triads (pages 44-45)

No. ____ ; key _____ ; M.M. _____ ; S / T

No. ____ ; key _____ ; M.M. _____ ; S / T

C. Prepared Sightreading Piece

What is the time signature? _____

How will you count it? say ____ ____ ____

Play daily without stopping, keeping a steady beat.

Circle any mistakes when you have finished.
Repeat until you play it perfectly.

____ on C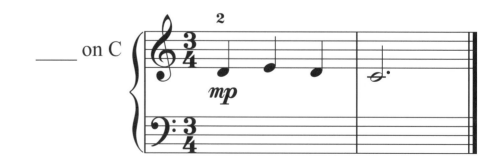

D. Aural Skills - Rhythmic

1)

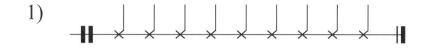

Turn the metronome on at M.M. ♩ = 60

  a) Clap with it.

  b) Turn it off, and clap at the same tempo
     without the metronome.

  c) Turn it on again and check yourself.
     Did you keep the same speed?

2)

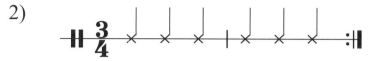

Tap/Clap this rhythm. Tap your knees with
both hands on beat 1; clap on beats 2 and 3.

3)

Compare this example to the Prepared Sightreading Piece.

  a) Write in the missing beats to match its rhythm.

  b) Clap the completed rhythm while counting out loud;
     clap it again from memory.

E. Aural Skills - Pitch

1)

  a) Draw lines connecting the notes above.

  b) What is the distance between each note?
     Fill in the blanks with your answers.

     Tip: Check "How to Use This Book"
        if you're not sure what to write.

2)

  a) Play this motif, starting on any finger.

  b) Play again. Sing along as you play.

     Tip: You may have to slide your voice
        around to find the first note!

  c) Play and sing again – but this time
     don't play the last note, just sing it.

Unit 1 - Module 2

A. Brainthumpers

Play these notes with the written fingering while counting out loud.
Practice daily.

1)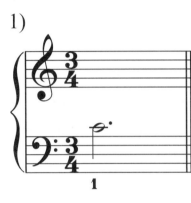

2)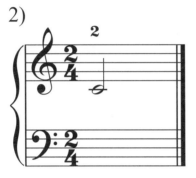

C. Prepared Sightreading Piece

What is the time signature? _____

How will you count it? say _____ _____ _____ _____

Play daily without stopping, keeping a steady beat.

Circle any mistakes when you have finished.
Repeat until you play it perfectly.

_____ on B

D. Aural Skills - Rhythmic

1)

Turn the metronome on at M.M. ♩ = 80

   a) Clap with it.

   b) Turn it off, and clap at the same tempo
      without the metronome.

   c) Turn it on again and check yourself.
      Did you keep the same speed?

2)

Tap/Clap this rhythm. Tap your knees with
both hands on beat 1; clap on beats 2, 3 and 4.

3)

Compare this example to the Prepared Sightreading Piece.

   a) Write in the missing beats to match its rhythm.

   b) Clap the completed rhythm while counting out loud;
      clap it again from memory.

E. Aural Skills - Pitch

1)

   a) Draw lines connecting the notes above.

   b) What is the distance between each note?
      Fill in the blanks with your answers.

2)

   a) Play this motif, starting on any finger.

   b) Play again. Sing along as you play.
      *Tip: You may have to slide your voice
          around to find the first note!*

   c) Play and sing again – but this time
      don't play the last note, just sing it.

Unit 1 - Module 3

A. Brainthumpers

Play these notes with the written fingering while counting out loud.
Practice daily.

1) 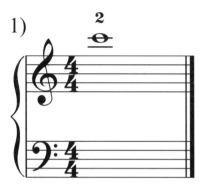   2)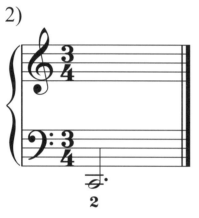

B. Technic

Practice daily, hands separate (S) or together (T).

1) Pentascales (pages 42-43)

    No. _____ ; key _____ ; M.M. _____ ; S / T

    No. _____ ; key _____ ; M.M. _____ ; S / T

2) Triads (pages 44-45)

    No. _____ ; key _____ ; M.M. _____ ; S / T

    No. _____ ; key _____ ; M.M. _____ ; S / T

C. Prepared Sightreading Piece

What is the time signature? _____

How will you count it? say ____ ____ ____ ____   _____ on D

Play daily without stopping, keeping a steady beat.

Circle any mistakes when you have finished.
Repeat until you play it perfectly.

D. Aural Skills - Rhythmic

1)

Turn the metronome on at M.M. ♩ = 100

   a) Clap with it.

   b) Turn it off, and clap at the same tempo
      without the metronome.

   c) Turn it on again and check yourself.
      Did you keep the same speed?

2)

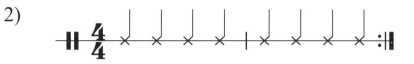

Tap/Clap this rhythm. Tap your knees with
both hands on beat 1; clap on beats 2, 3 and 4.

3)

Compare this example to the Prepared Sightreading Piece.

   a) Write in the missing beats to match its rhythm.

   b) Clap the completed rhythm while counting out loud;
      clap it again from memory.

E. Aural Skills - Pitch

1)

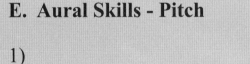

   a) Draw lines connecting the notes above.

   b) What is the distance between each note?
      Fill in the blanks with your answers.

2)

   a) Play this motif, starting on any finger.

   b) Play again. Sing along as you play.
      *Tip: You may have to slide your voice
         around to find the first note!*

   c) Play and sing again – but this time
      don't play the last note, just sing it.

A. Brainthumpers

Play these notes with the written fingering while counting out loud. Practice daily.

1)
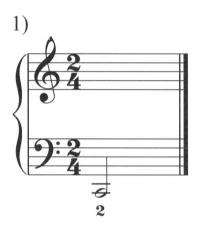

2)
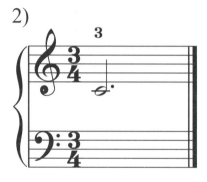

B. Technic

Practice daily, hands separate (S) or together (T).

1) Pentascales (pages 42-43)

No. _____ ; key _____ ; M.M. _____ ; S / T

No. _____ ; key _____ ; M.M. _____ ; S / T

2) Triads (pages 44-45)

No. _____ ; key _____ ; M.M. _____ ; S / T

No. _____ ; key _____ ; M.M. _____ ; S / T

C. Prepared Sightreading Piece

What is the time signature? _____

How will you count it? say ____ ____ ____

Play daily without stopping, keeping a steady beat.

Circle any mistakes when you have finished.
Repeat until you play it perfectly.

_____ on B
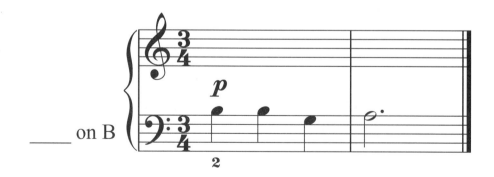

D. Aural Skills - Rhythmic

1)

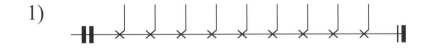

2)

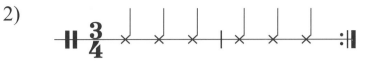

Turn the metronome on at M.M. ♩ = 63

Tap/Clap this rhythm. Tap your knees with both hands on beat 1; clap on beats 2 and 3.

   a) Clap with it.

   b) Turn it off, and clap at the same tempo without the metronome.

   c) Turn it on again and check yourself. Did you keep the same speed?

3)

Compare this example to the Prepared Sightreading Piece.

   a) Write in the missing beats to match its rhythm.

   b) Clap the completed rhythm while counting out loud; clap it again from memory.

E. Aural Skills - Pitch

1)

   a) Draw lines connecting the notes above.

   b) What is the distance between each note? Fill in the blanks with your answers.

2)

   a) Play this motif, starting on any finger.

   b) Play again. Sing along as you play.
     Tip: You may have to slide your voice around to find the first note!

   c) Play and sing again – but this time don't play the last note, just sing it.

A. Brainthumpers

Play these notes with the written fingering while counting out loud.
Practice daily.

1)

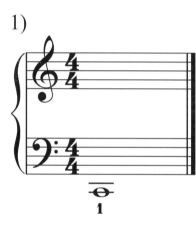

2)

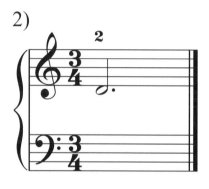

B. Technic

Practice daily, hands separate (S) or together (T).

1) Pentascales (for exercises written out in all keys, see the Technic Book)

No. _____; key _____; M.M. _____; S / T

No. _____; key _____; M.M. _____; S / T

2) Triads (for exercises written out in all keys, see the Technic Book)

No. _____; key _____; M.M. _____; S / T

No. _____; key _____; M.M. _____; S / T

C. Prepared Sightreading Piece

What is the time signature? _____

How will you count it? say ____ ____ ____ ____

_____ on G

Play daily without stopping, keeping a steady beat.

Circle any mistakes when you have finished.
Repeat until you play it perfectly.

D. Aural Skills - Rhythmic

1)

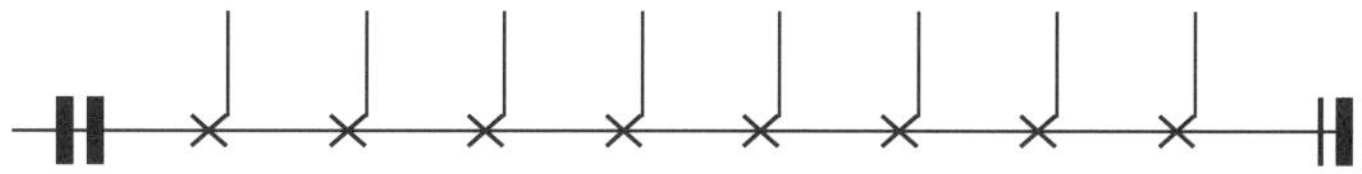

Turn the metronome on at M.M. ♩= 72

a) Clap with it.

b) Turn it off, and clap at the same tempo without the metronome.

c) Turn it on again and check yourself. Did you keep the same speed?

2)

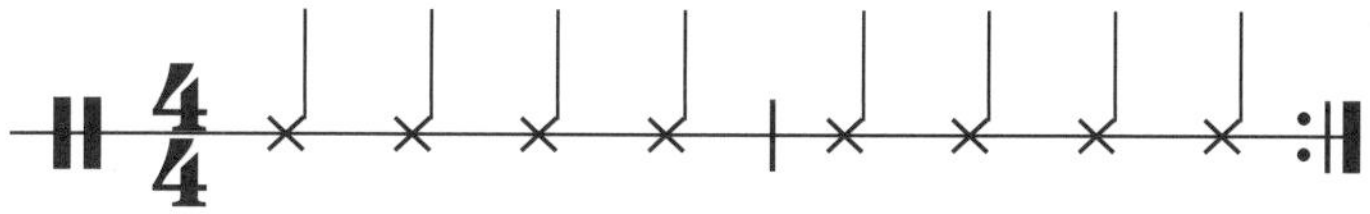

Tap/Clap this rhythm. Tap your knees with both hands on beat 1; clap on beats 2, 3 and 4.

3)

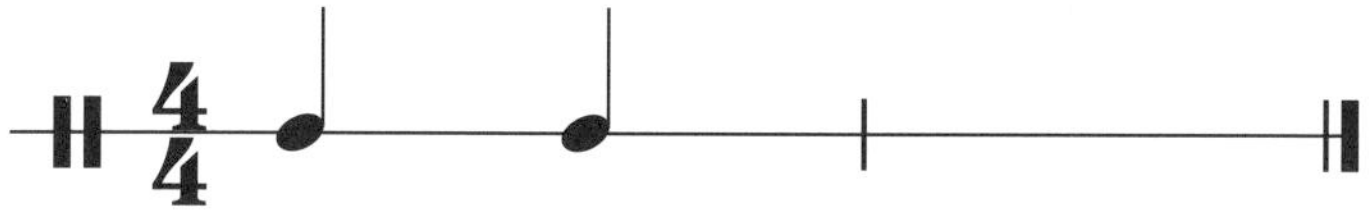

Compare this example to the Prepared Sightreading Piece.

a) Write in the missing beats to match its rhythm.

b) Clap the completed rhythm while counting out loud; clap it again from memory.

E. Aural Skills - Pitch

1)

____ ____ ____

a) Draw lines connecting the notes above.

b) What is the distance between each note? Fill in the blanks with your answers.

Tip: Check "How to Use This Book" if you're not sure what to write.

2)

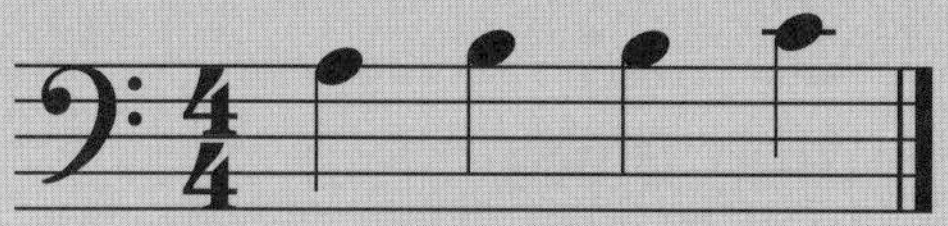

a) Play this motif, starting on any finger.

b) Play again. Sing along as you play.

Tip: You may have to slide your voice around to find the first note!

c) Play and sing again – but this time don't play the last note, just sing it.

Unit 2 - Module 2

A. Brainthumpers

Play these notes with the written fingering while counting out loud. Practice daily.

1) 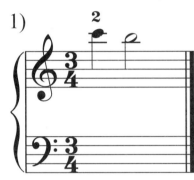   2)

B. Technic

Practice daily, hands separate (S) or together (T).

1) Pentascales (for exercises written out in all keys, see the Technic Book)

No. _____; key _____; M.M. _____; S / T

No. _____; key _____; M.M. _____; S / T

2) Triads (for exercises written out in all keys, see the Technic Book)

No. _____; key _____; M.M. _____; S / T

No. _____; key _____; M.M. _____; S / T

C. Prepared Sightreading Piece

What is the time signature? _____

How will you count it? say ____ ____ ____ ____   _____ on D

Play daily without stopping, keeping a steady beat.

Circle any mistakes when you have finished.
Repeat until you play it perfectly.

D. Aural Skills - Rhythmic

1)

Turn the metronome on at M.M. ♩ = 50

   a) Clap with it.

   b) Turn it off, and clap at the same tempo
      without the metronome.

   c) Turn it on again and check yourself.
      Did you keep the same speed?

2)

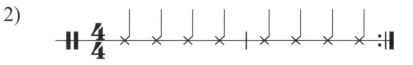

Tap/Clap this rhythm. Tap your knees with
both hands on beat 1; clap on beats 2, 3 and 4.

3)

Compare this example to the Prepared Sightreading Piece.

   a) Write in the missing beats to match its rhythm.

   b) Clap the completed rhythm while counting out loud;
      clap it again from memory.

E. Aural Skills - Pitch

1)

   a) Draw lines connecting the notes above.

   b) What is the distance between each note?
      Fill in the blanks with your answers.

2)

   a) Play this motif, starting on any finger.

   b) Play again. Sing along as you play.
      *Tip: You may have to slide your voice
           around to find the first note!*

   c) Play and sing again – but this time
      don't play the last note, just sing it.

A. Brainthumpers

Play these notes with the written fingering while counting out loud.
Practice daily.

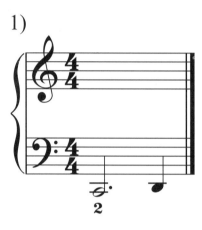

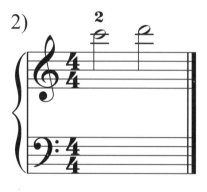

C. Prepared Sightreading Piece

What is the time signature? _____

How will you count it? say ____ ____ ____ ____

Play daily without stopping, keeping a steady beat.

Circle any mistakes when you have finished.
Repeat until you play it perfectly.

_____ on C

D. Aural Skills - Rhythmic

1)

Turn the metronome on at M.M. ♩ = 96

    a) Clap with it.

    b) Turn it off, and clap at the same tempo
       without the metronome.

    c) Turn it on again and check yourself.
       Did you keep the same speed?

2)

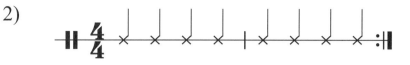

Tap/Clap this rhythm. Tap your knees with
both hands on beat 1; clap on beats 2, 3 and 4.

3)

Compare this example to the Prepared Sightreading Piece.

    a) Write in the missing beats to match its rhythm.

    b) Clap the completed rhythm while counting out loud;
       clap it again from memory.

E. Aural Skills - Pitch

1)

_____   _____   _____

    a) Draw lines connecting the notes above.

    b) What is the distance between each note?
       Fill in the blanks with your answers.

2)

    a) Play this motif, starting on any finger.

    b) Play again. Sing along as you play.
       *Tip: You may have to slide your voice
          around to find the first note!*

    c) Play and sing again – but this time
       don't play the last note, just sing it.

A. Brainthumpers

Play these notes with the written fingering while counting out loud.
Practice daily.

1)

2)

B. Technic

Practice daily, hands separate (S) or together (T).

1) Pentascales (for exercises written out in all keys, see the Technic Book)

No. _____ ; key _____ ; M.M. _____ ; S / T

No. _____ ; key _____ ; M.M. _____ ; S / T

2) Triads (for exercises written out in all keys, see the Technic Book)

No. _____ ; key _____ ; M.M. _____ ; S / T

No. _____ ; key _____ ; M.M. _____ ; S / T

C. Prepared Sightreading Piece

What is the time signature? _____

How will you count it? say _____ _____ _____ _____ _____ on F

Play daily without stopping, keeping a steady beat.

Circle any mistakes when you have finished.
Repeat until you play it perfectly.

17

D. Aural Skills - Rhythmic

1)

Turn the metronome on at M.M. ♩ = 84

   a) Clap with it.

   b) Turn it off, and clap at the same tempo
      without the metronome.

   c) Turn it on again and check yourself.
      Did you keep the same speed?

2)

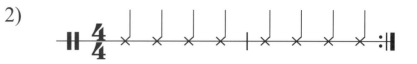

Tap/Clap this rhythm. Tap your knees with
both hands on beat 1; clap on beats 2, 3 and 4.

3)

Compare this example to the Prepared Sightreading Piece.

   a) Write in the missing beats to match its rhythm.

   b) Clap the completed rhythm while counting out loud;
      clap it again from memory.

E. Aural Skills - Pitch

1)

   a) Draw lines connecting the notes above.

   b) What is the distance between each note?
      Fill in the blanks with your answers.

2)

   a) Play this motif, starting on any finger.

   b) Play again. Sing along as you play.
      *Tip: You may have to slide your voice
      around to find the first note!*

   c) Play and sing again – but this time
      don't play the last note, just sing it.

A. Brainthumpers

Play these notes with the written fingering while counting out loud.
Practice daily.

1)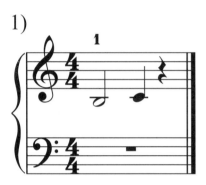

2)

B. Technic

Practice daily, hands separate (S) or together (T).

1) Pentascales (for exercises written out in all keys, see the Technic Book)

No. ____; key _____; M.M. _____; S / T

No. ____; key _____; M.M. _____; S / T

2) Triads (for exercises written out in all keys, see the Technic Book)

No. ____; key _____; M.M. _____; S / T

No. ____; key _____; M.M. _____; S / T

C. Prepared Sightreading Piece

What is the time signature? _____

How will you count it? say ____ ____ ____ ____   ____ on F

Play daily without stopping, keeping a steady beat.

Circle any mistakes when you have finished.
Repeat until you play it perfectly.

D. Aural Skills - Rhythmic

1)

Turn the metronome on at M.M. ♩ = 60

    a) Listen to the metronome for four beats.

    b) Clap with the metronome for four beats
       without pausing.

Do this three times.

2)
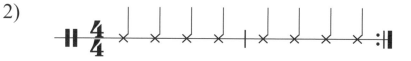

Tap/Clap this rhythm. Tap your knees with
both hands on beat 1; clap on beats 2, 3 and 4.

3)

Compare this example to the Prepared Sightreading Piece.

    a) Write in the missing beats to match its rhythm.

    b) Clap the completed rhythm while counting out loud;
       clap it again from memory.

E. Aural Skills - Pitch

1)

———   ———   ———

    a) Draw lines connecting the notes above.

    b) What is the distance between each note?
       Fill in the blanks with your answers.

       Tip: Check "How to Use This Book"
       if you're not sure what to write.

2)

    a) Play this motif, starting on any finger.

    b) Play again. Sing along as you play.

       Tip: You may have to slide your voice
       around to find the first note!

    c) Play and sing again – but this time
       don't play the last note, just sing it.

A. Brainthumpers

Play these notes with the written fingering while counting out loud.
Practice daily.

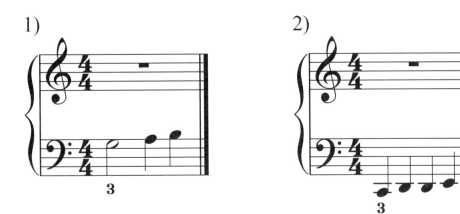

1)

2)

B. Technic

Practice daily, hands separate (S) or together (T).

1) Pentascales (for exercises written out in all keys, see the Technic Book)

No. _____ ; key _____ ; M.M. _____ ; S / T

No. _____ ; key _____ ; M.M. _____ ; S / T

2) Triads (for exercises written out in all keys, see the Technic Book)

No. _____ ; key _____ ; M.M. _____ ; S / T

No. _____ ; key _____ ; M.M. _____ ; S / T

C. Prepared Sightreading Piece

What is the time signature? _____

How will you count it? say _____ _____ _____

Play daily without stopping, keeping a steady beat.

Circle any mistakes when you have finished.
Repeat until you play it perfectly.

_____ on C

D. Aural Skills - Rhythmic

1)

Turn the metronome on at M.M. ♩ = 80

    a) Listen to the metronome for three beats.

    b) Clap with the metronome for three beats
       without pausing.

Do this three times.

2)

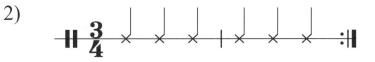

Tap/Clap this rhythm. Tap your knees with
both hands on beat 1; clap on beats 2 and 3.

3)

Compare this example to the Prepared Sightreading Piece.

    a) Write in the missing beats to match its rhythm.

    b) Clap the completed rhythm while counting out loud;
       clap it again from memory.

E. Aural Skills - Pitch

1)

    a) Draw lines connecting the notes above.

    b) What is the distance between each note?
       Fill in the blanks with your answers.

2)

    a) Play this motif, starting on any finger.

    b) Play again. Sing along as you play.
       *Tip: You may have to slide your voice
          around to find the first note!*

    c) Play and sing again – but this time
       don't play the last note, just sing it.

A. Brainthumpers

Play these notes with the written fingering while counting out loud.
Practice daily.

1)
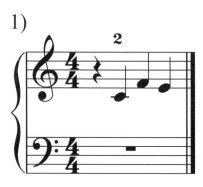

2)
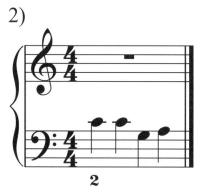

B. Technic

Practice daily, hands separate (S) or together (T).

1) Pentascales (for exercises written out in all keys, see the Technic Book)

    No. ____; key _____; M.M. _____; S / T

    No. ____; key _____; M.M. _____; S / T

2) Triads (for exercises written out in all keys, see the Technic Book)

    No. ____; key _____; M.M. _____; S / T

    No. ____; key _____; M.M. _____; S / T

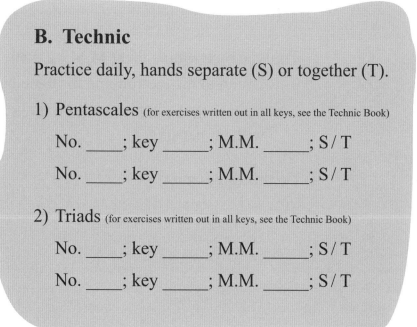

C. Prepared Sightreading Piece

What is the time signature? _____

How will you count it? say ____ ____ ____ ____

Play daily without stopping, keeping a steady beat.

Circle any mistakes when you have finished.
Repeat until you play it perfectly.

____ on C

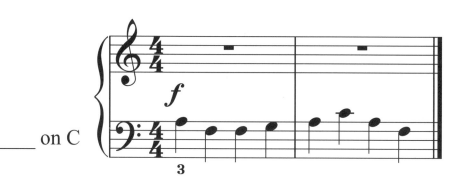

D. Aural Skills - Rhythmic

1)

Turn the metronome on at M.M. ♩ = 92

    a) Listen to the metronome for four beats.

    b) Clap with the metronome for four beats
       without pausing.

Do this three times.

2)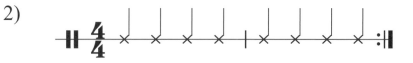

Tap/Clap this rhythm. Tap your knees with both hands on beat 1; clap on beats 2, 3 and 4.

3)

Compare this example to the Prepared Sightreading Piece.

    a) Write in the missing beats to match its rhythm.

    b) Clap the completed rhythm while counting out loud;
       clap it again from memory.

E. Aural Skills - Pitch

1)

_____   _____   _____

    a) Draw lines connecting the notes above.

    b) What is the distance between each note?
       Fill in the blanks with your answers.

2)

    a) Play this motif, starting on any finger.

    b) Play again. Sing along as you play.
       *Tip: You may have to slide your voice
           around to find the first note!*

    c) Play and sing again – but this time
       don't play the last note, just sing it.

A. Brainthumpers

Play these notes with the written fingering while counting out loud. Practice daily.

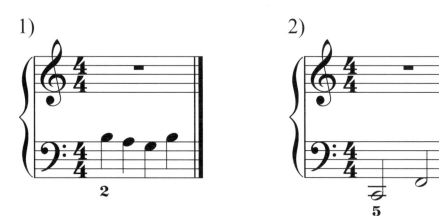

1)

2)

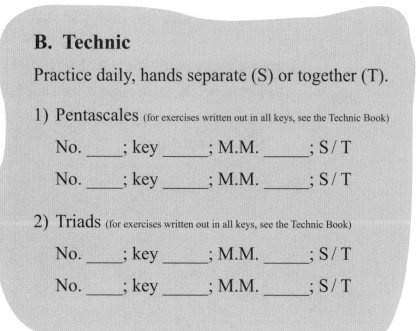

B. Technic

Practice daily, hands separate (S) or together (T).

1) Pentascales (for exercises written out in all keys, see the Technic Book)

No. _____; key _____; M.M. _____; S / T

No. _____; key _____; M.M. _____; S / T

2) Triads (for exercises written out in all keys, see the Technic Book)

No. _____; key _____; M.M. _____; S / T

No. _____; key _____; M.M. _____; S / T

C. Prepared Sightreading Piece

What is the time signature? _____

How will you count it? say ____ ____ ____ ____

Play daily without stopping, keeping a steady beat.

Circle any mistakes when you have finished.
Repeat until you play it perfectly.

_____ on A

D. Aural Skills - Rhythmic

1)

Turn the metronome on at M.M. ♩ = 72

   a) Listen to the metronome for four beats.

   b) Clap with the metronome for four beats
      without pausing.

Do this three times.

2)

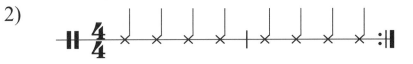

Tap/Clap this rhythm. Tap your knees with
both hands on beat 1; clap on beats 2, 3 and 4.

3)

Compare this example to the Prepared Sightreading Piece.

   a) Write in the missing beats to match its rhythm.

   b) Clap the completed rhythm while counting out loud;
      clap it again from memory.

E. Aural Skills - Pitch

1)

   a) Draw lines connecting the notes above.

   b) What is the distance between each note?
      Fill in the blanks with your answers.

2)

   a) Play this motif, starting on any finger.

   b) Play again. Sing along as you play.
      *Tip: You may have to slide your voice
         around to find the first note!*

   c) Play and sing again – but this time
      don't play the last note, just sing it.

A. Brainthumpers

Play these notes with the written fingering while counting out loud.
Practice daily.

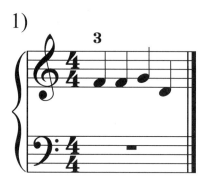

C. Prepared Sightreading Piece

What is the time signature? _____

How will you count it? say ____ ____ ____

Play daily without stopping, keeping a steady beat.

Circle any mistakes when you have finished.
Repeat until you play it perfectly.

_____ on F

D. Aural Skills - Rhythmic

1)

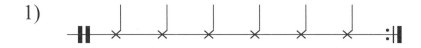

Turn the metronome on at M.M. ♩ = 100

   a) Listen to the metronome for three beats.

   b) Clap with the metronome for three beats
      without pausing.

Do this three times.

2)

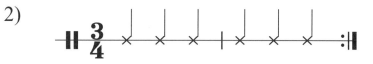

Tap/Clap this rhythm. Tap your knees with
both hands on beat 1; clap on beats 2 and 3.

3)

Compare this example to the Prepared Sightreading Piece.

   a) Write in the missing beats to match its rhythm.

   b) Clap the completed rhythm while counting out loud;
      clap it again from memory.

E. Aural Skills - Pitch

1)

_____ _____ _____

   a) Draw lines connecting the notes above.

   b) What is the distance between each note?
      Fill in the blanks with your answers.

    *Tip: Check "How to Use This Book"
      if you're not sure what to write.*

2)

   a) Play this motif, starting on any finger.

   b) Play again. Sing along as you play.
    *Tip: You may have to slide your voice
      around to find the first note!*

   c) Play and sing again – but this time
      don't play the last note, just sing it.

A. Brainthumpers

Play these notes with the written fingering while counting out loud.
Practice daily.

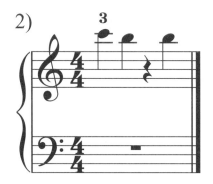

C. Prepared Sightreading Piece

What is the time signature? _____

How will you count it? say ____ ____ ____ ____

Play daily without stopping, keeping a steady beat.

Circle any mistakes when you have finished.
Repeat until you play it perfectly.

_____ on E

D. Aural Skills - Rhythmic

1)

Turn the metronome on at M.M. ♩ = 76

   a) Listen to the metronome for four beats.

   b) Clap with the metronome for four beats
      without pausing.

Do this three times.

2)

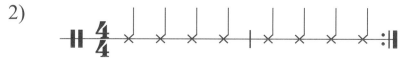

Tap/Clap this rhythm. Tap your knees with
both hands on beat 1; clap on beats 2, 3 and 4.

3)

Compare this example to the Prepared Sightreading Piece.

   a) Write in the missing beats to match its rhythm.

   b) Clap the completed rhythm while counting out loud;
      clap it again from memory.

E. Aural Skills - Pitch

1)

   a) Draw lines connecting the notes above.

   b) What is the distance between each note?
      Fill in the blanks with your answers.

2)

   a) Play this motif, starting on any finger.

   b) Play again. Sing along as you play.
      *Tip: You may have to slide your voice
         around to find the first note!*

   c) Play and sing again – but this time
      don't play the last note, just sing it.

Unit 4 - Module 3

A. Brainthumpers

Play these notes with the written fingering while counting out loud. Practice daily.

1)
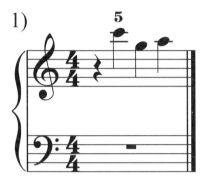

2)
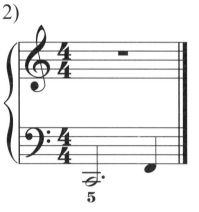

B. Technic

Practice daily, hands separate (S) or together (T).

1) Pentascales (for exercises written out in all keys, see the Technic Book)

No. ____ ; key _____ ; M.M. _____ ; S / T

No. ____ ; key _____ ; M.M. _____ ; S / T

2) Triads (for exercises written out in all keys, see the Technic Book)

No. ____ ; key _____ ; M.M. _____ ; S / T

No. ____ ; key _____ ; M.M. _____ ; S / T

C. Prepared Sightreading Piece

What is the time signature? _____

How will you count it? say ____ ____ ____

Play daily without stopping, keeping a steady beat.

Circle any mistakes when you have finished.
Repeat until you play it perfectly.

____ on C
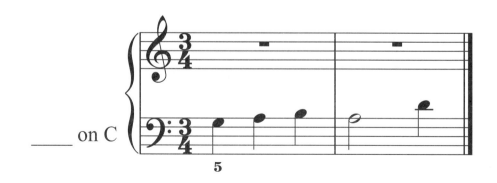

D. Aural Skills - Rhythmic

1)

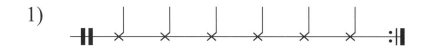

Turn the metronome on at M.M. ♩ = 88

   a) Listen to the metronome for three beats.

   b) Clap with the metronome for three beats
      without pausing.

Do this three times.

2)

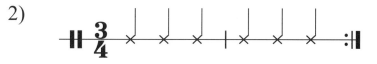

Tap/Clap this rhythm. Tap your knees with
both hands on beat 1; clap on beats 2 and 3.

3)

Compare this example to the Prepared Sightreading Piece.

   a) Write in the missing beats to match its rhythm.

   b) Clap the completed rhythm while counting out loud;
      clap it again from memory.

E. Aural Skills - Pitch

1)

_____ _____

   a) Draw lines connecting the notes above.

   b) What is the distance between each note?
      Fill in the blanks with your answers.

2)

   a) Play this motif, starting on any finger.

   b) Play again. Sing along as you play.
      *Tip: You may have to slide your voice
           around to find the first note!*

   c) Play and sing again – but this time
      don't play the last note, just sing it.

A. Brainthumpers

Play these notes with the written fingering while counting out loud.
Practice daily.

1)

2)

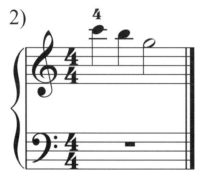

C. Prepared Sightreading Piece

What is the time signature? _____

How will you count it? say ____ ____ ____ ____   ____ on D

Play daily without stopping, keeping a steady beat.

Circle any mistakes when you have finished.
Repeat until you play it perfectly.

D. Aural Skills - Rhythmic

1)

Turn the metronome on at M.M. ♩ = 92

  a) Listen to the metronome for four beats.

  b) Clap with the metronome for four beats
     without pausing.

Do this three times.

2)

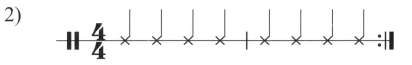

Tap/Clap this rhythm. Tap your knees with
both hands on beat 1; clap on beats 2, 3 and 4.

3)

Compare this example to the Prepared Sightreading Piece.

  a) Write in the missing beats to match its rhythm.

  b) Clap the completed rhythm while counting out loud;
     clap it again from memory.

E. Aural Skills - Pitch

1)

  a) Draw lines connecting the notes above.

  b) What is the distance between each note?
     Fill in the blanks with your answers.

2)

  a) Play this motif, starting on any finger.

  b) Play again. Sing along as you play.
     *Tip: You may have to slide your voice
         around to find the first note!*

  c) Play and sing again – but this time
     don't play the last note, just sing it.

Unit 1 - Midterm

I. Technic   Grade ☐

Student to play pentascale: **No(s).** _____ ; **key(s)** _____ ; **M.M.** _____

Student to play triad: **No(s).** _____ ; **key(s)** _____ ; **M.M.** _____

II. Sightreading   Grade ☐

1. Student may study for up to 15 seconds.
2. Student then plays:

1

Sightreading Skills Check

Notes	Fingering
Rhythm	Dynamics
Steady Tempo	Other

III. Aural Skills - Rhythmic   Grade ☐

Student should face away from keyboard. Each element may be played twice.

A. Beat Clap-Along

Play the student part of *Calvado* (*APP* Repertoire Album, p. 16). Ask student to clap the beat as you play, joining in after a few beats.

B. Echo Clap

Play and ask the student to clap back the rhythmic pattern. Note lengths should be accurate and the tempo steady.

IV. Aural Skills - Pitch   Grade ☐

Student should face away from the keyboard. Each element may be played twice.

A. High-Low Identification

Play and ask the student if the second note is higher in pitch than the first.

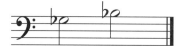

B. Echo-Sing

1. Play first note and ask student to match with voice.
2. Play complete example and ask student to sing. Pitch and rhythm should both be accurate.

C. Melody-Completion

Play an A minor triad. Play the Sightreading example (section II).
Play again leaving out the last note. Student sings the missing last note.
Pitch should be accurate.

Unit 1 - Final

I. Technic   Grade [　　]

Student to play pentascale: **No(s).** _____ ; **key(s)** _____ ; **M.M.** _____

Student to play triad: **No(s).** _____ ; **key(s)** _____ ; **M.M.** _____

II. Sightreading   Grade [　　]

1. Student may study for up to 15 seconds.
2. Student then plays:

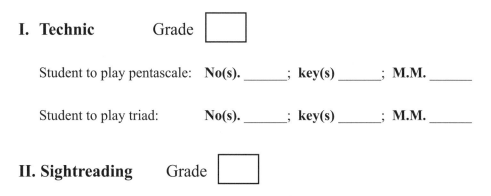

Sightreading Skills Check

Notes	Fingering
Rhythm	Dynamics
Steady Tempo	Other

III. Aural Skills - Rhythmic   Grade [　　]

Student should face away from keyboard. Each element may be played twice.

A. Beat Clap-Along

Play the student part of *Having a Lovely Time* (*APP* Repertoire Album, p. 26).
Ask student to clap the beat as you play, joining in after a few beats.

B. Echo Clap

Play and ask the student to clap back the rhythmic pattern. Note lengths
should be accurate and the tempo steady.

IV. Aural Skills - Pitch   Grade [　　]

Student should face away from the keyboard. Each element may be played twice.

A. High-Low Identification

Play and ask the student if the second note is lower in pitch than the first.

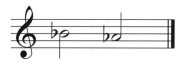

B. Echo-Sing

1. Play first note and ask student to match with voice.
2. Play complete example and ask student to sing. Pitch and rhythm should
   both be accurate.

C. Melody-Completion

Play a C major triad. Play the Sightreading example (section II).
Play again leaving out the last note. Student sings the missing last note.
Pitch should be accurate.

Unit 2 - Midterm

I. Technic   Grade ☐

Student to play pentascale: **No(s).** _____; **key(s)** _____; **M.M.** _____

Student to play triad: **No(s).** _____; **key(s)** _____; **M.M.** _____

II. Sightreading   Grade ☐

1. Student may study for up to 15 seconds.
2. Student then plays:

Sightreading Skills Check

Notes	Fingering
Rhythm	Dynamics
Steady Tempo	Other

III. Aural Skills - Rhythmic   Grade ☐

Student should face away from keyboard. Each element may be played twice.

A. Beat Clap-Along

Play the student part of *Around the Clock* (*APP* Repertoire Album, p. 30). Ask student to clap the beat as you play, joining in after a few beats.

B. Echo Clap

Play and ask the student to clap back the rhythmic pattern. Note lengths should be accurate and the tempo steady.

IV. Aural Skills - Pitch   Grade ☐

Student should face away from the keyboard. Each element may be played twice.

A. High-Low Identification

Play and ask the student if the second note is lower in pitch than the first.

B. Echo-Sing

1. Play first note and ask student to match with voice.
2. Play complete example and ask student to sing. Pitch and rhythm should both be accurate.

C. Melody-Completion

Play a C major triad. Play the Sightreading example (section II. above). Play again leaving out the last note. Student sings the missing last note. Pitch should be accurate.

Unit 2 - Final

I. Technic   Grade [ ]

Student to play pentascale: **No(s).** _____ ; **key(s)** _____ ; **M.M.** _____

Student to play triad: **No(s).** _____ ; **key(s)** _____ ; **M.M.** _____

II. Sightreading   Grade [ ]

1. Student may study for up to 15 seconds.
2. Student then plays:

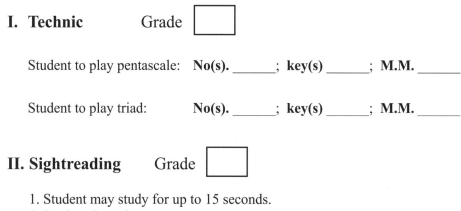

Sightreading Skills Check

Notes	Fingering
Rhythm	Dynamics
Steady Tempo	Other

III. Aural Skills - Rhythmic   Grade [ ]

Student should face away from keyboard. Each element may be played twice.

A. Beat Clap-Along

Play the student part of *Still Dreaming* (*APP* Repertoire Album, p. 24). Ask student to clap the beat as you play, joining in after a few beats.

B. Echo Clap

Play and ask the student to clap back the rhythmic pattern. Note lengths should be accurate and the tempo steady.

IV. Aural Skills - Pitch   Grade [ ]

Student should face away from the keyboard. Each element may be played twice.

A. High-Low Identification

Play and ask the student if the second note is higher in pitch than the first.

B. Echo-Sing

1. Play first note and ask student to match with voice.
2. Play complete example and ask student to sing. Pitch and rhythm should both be accurate.

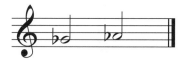

C. Melody-Completion

Play a C major triad. Play the Sightreading example (section II. above). Play again leaving out the last note. Student sings the missing last note. Pitch should be accurate.

Unit 3 - Midterm

I. Technic   Grade ☐

Student to play pentascale: **No(s).** _____; **key(s)** _____; **M.M.** _____

Student to play triad: **No(s).** _____; **key(s)** _____; **M.M.** _____

II. Sightreading   Grade ☐

1. Student may study for up to 15 seconds.
2. Student then plays:

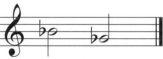

2

Sightreading Skills Check

Notes	Fingering
Rhythm	Dynamics
Steady Tempo	Other

III. Aural Skills - Rhythmic   Grade ☐

Student should face away from keyboard. Each element may be played twice.

A. Beat Clap-Along

Play the student part of *London Waltz* (*APP* Repertoire Album, p. 12). Ask student to clap the beat as you play, joining in after a few beats.

B. Echo Clap

Play and ask the student to clap back the rhythmic pattern. Note lengths should be accurate and the tempo steady.

IV. Aural Skills - Pitch   Grade ☐

Student should face away from the keyboard. Each element may be played twice.

A. High-Low Identification

Play and ask the student if the second note is higher in pitch than the first.

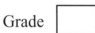

B. Echo-Sing

1. Play first note and ask student to match with voice.
2. Play complete example and ask student to sing. Pitch and rhythm should both be accurate.

C. Melody-Completion

Play a G major triad. Play the Sightreading example (section II. above). Play again leaving out the last note. Student sings the missing last note. Pitch should be accurate.

Unit 3 - Final

I. Technic   Grade ☐

Student to play pentascale: **No(s).** _____; **key(s)** _____; **M.M.** _____

Student to play triad: **No(s).** _____; **key(s)** _____; **M.M.** _____

II. Sightreading   Grade ☐

1. Student may study for up to 15 seconds.
2. Student then plays:

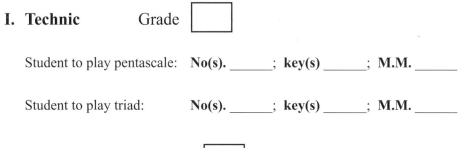

Sightreading Skills Check

Notes	Fingering
Rhythm	Dynamics
Steady Tempo	Other

III. Aural Skills - Rhythmic   Grade ☐

Student should face away from keyboard. Each element may be played twice.

A. Beat Clap-Along

Play the student part of *June Days* (*APP* Repertoire Album, p. 22). Ask student to clap the beat as you play, joining in after a few beats.

B. Echo Clap

Play and ask the student to clap back the rhythmic pattern. Note lengths should be accurate and the tempo steady.

IV. Aural Skills - Pitch   Grade ☐

Student should face away from the keyboard. Each element may be played twice.

A. High-Low Identification

Play and ask the student if the first note is lower in pitch than the second.

B. Echo-Sing

1. Play first note and ask student to match with voice.
2. Play complete example and ask student to sing. Pitch and rhythm should both be accurate.

C. Melody-Completion

Play a G major triad. Play the Sightreading example (section II. above). Play again leaving out the last note. Student sings the missing last note. Pitch should be accurate.

Unit 4 - Midterm

I. Technic   Grade [ ]

Student to play pentascale: **No(s).** _____; **key(s)** _____; **M.M.** _____

Student to play triad: **No(s).** _____; **key(s)** _____; **M.M.** _____

II. Sightreading   Grade [ ]

1. Student may study for up to 15 seconds.
2. Student then plays:

Sightreading Skills Check

Notes	Fingering
Rhythm	Dynamics
Steady Tempo	Other

III. Aural Skills - Rhythmic   Grade [ ]

Student should face away from keyboard. Each element may be played twice.

A. Beat Clap-Along

Play the student part of *Leave Me Alone* (*APP* Repertoire Album, p. 36). Ask student to clap the beat as you play, joining in after a few beats.

B. Echo Clap

Play and ask the student to clap back the rhythmic pattern. Note lengths should be accurate and the tempo steady.

IV. Aural Skills - Pitch   Grade [ ]

Student should face away from the keyboard. Each element may be played twice.

A. High-Low Identification

Play and ask the student if the second note is lower in pitch than the first.

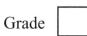

B. Echo-Sing

1. Play first note and ask student to match with voice.
2. Play complete example and ask student to sing. Pitch and rhythm should both be accurate.

C. Melody-Completion

Play a C major triad. Play the Sightreading example (section II. above). Play again leaving out the last note. Student sings the missing last note. Pitch should be accurate.

Unit 4 - Final

I. Technic   Grade [ ]

Student to play pentascale: **No(s).** _____ ; **key(s)** _____ ; **M.M.** _____

Student to play triad: **No(s).** _____ ; **key(s)** _____ ; **M.M.** _____

II. Sightreading   Grade [ ]

1. Student may study for up to 15 seconds.
2. Student then plays:

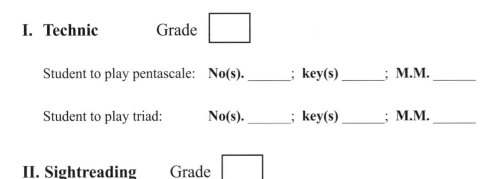

Sightreading Skills Check

Notes	Fingering
Rhythm	Dynamics
Steady Tempo	Other

III. Aural Skills - Rhythmic   Grade [ ]

Student should face away from keyboard. Each element may be played twice.

A. Beat Clap-Along

Play the student part of *Still My Favorite* (*APP* Repertoire Album, p. 6). Ask student to clap the beat as you play, joining in after a few beats.

B. Echo Clap

Play and ask the student to clap back the rhythmic pattern. Note lengths should be accurate and the tempo steady.

IV. Aural Skills - Pitch   Grade [ ]

Student should face away from the keyboard. Each element may be played twice.

A. High-Low Identification

Play and ask the student if the second note is higher in pitch than the first.

B. Echo-Sing

1. Play first note and ask student to match with voice.
2. Play complete example and ask student to sing. Pitch and rhythm should both be accurate.

C. Melody-Completion

Play a C major triad. Play the Sightreading example (section II. above). Play again leaving out the last note. Student sings the missing last note. Pitch should be accurate.

Prep Level Pentascales

Prepare in keys:
C F G Major
D E A Major

No. 1

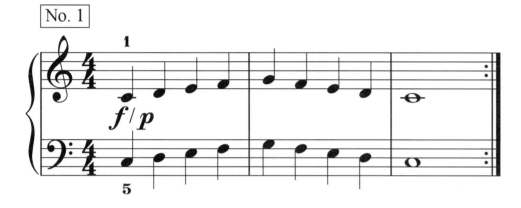

No. 2

No. 3

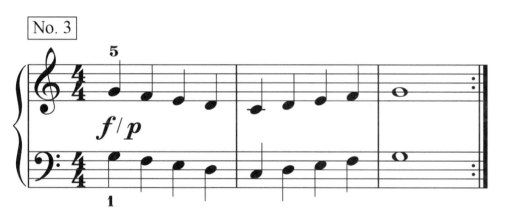

No. 4

No. 5

No. 6

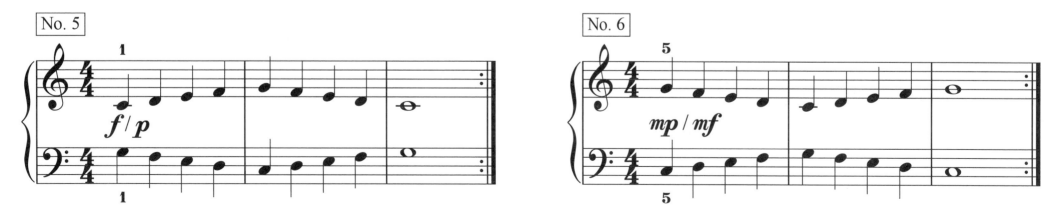

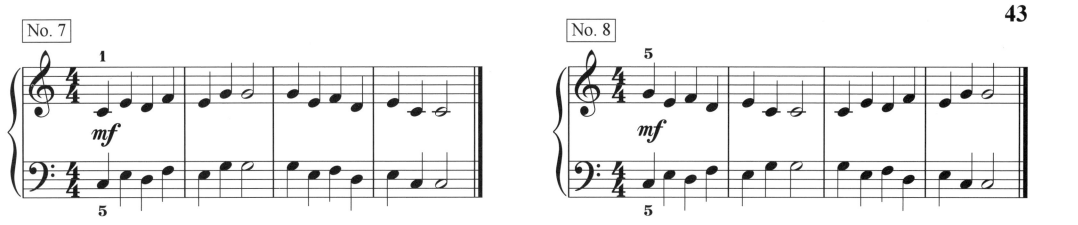

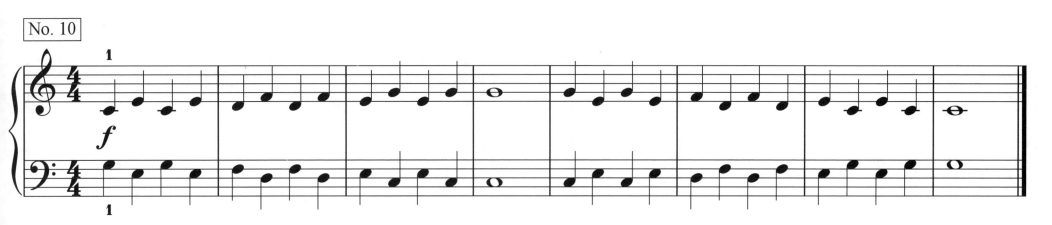

43

44

Prep Level Triads

Prepare in keys:
C F G Major
D E A Major

No. 1

No. 2

No. 3

No. 4

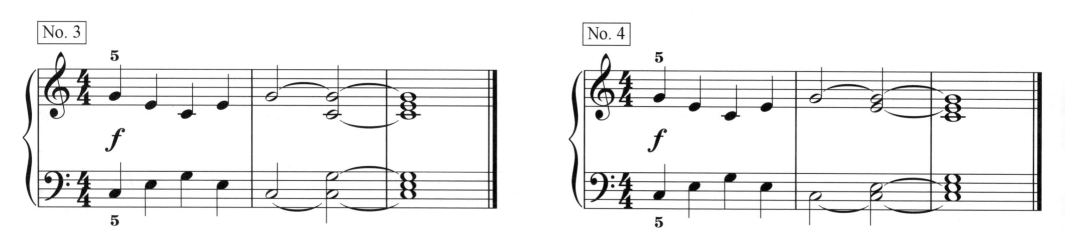

No. 5

No. 6

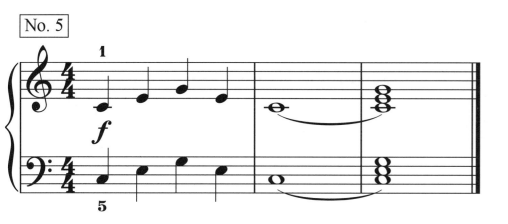

No. 7

No. 8

No. 9

No. 10

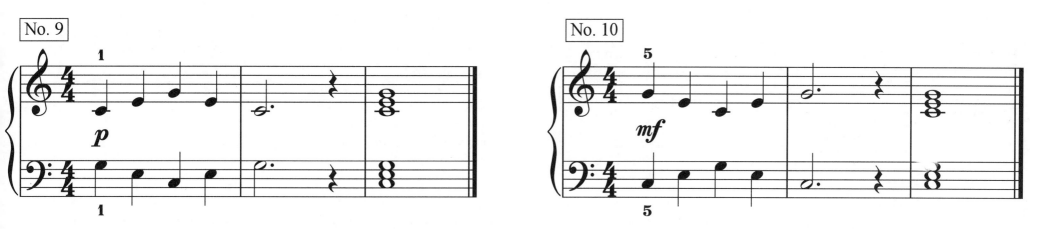

The *American Popular Piano Skills* books are designed to be used as a flexible tool for learning the fundamental skills of playing the piano.

Research tells us that the most effective way to learn is in small increments, repeated frequently. That's a good thing, considering that many piano students today have very busy schedules and may not have big chunks of time to devote to practice at one time.

American Popular Piano
Skills Book-Preparatory

Four Learning Units		**Four Examination Units**	
to be done by the student at home		to be administered by the teacher at the lesson	
Each Unit contains:		**Each Unit contains:**	
4 Learning Modules Each module covers the following skill areas:		**2 Tests** *Midterm:* to be completed after Module 2 *Final:* to be completed after Module 4	
Brainthumpers	Quick drills on notes, fingering and intervals	**Technic**	Pentascales, triads, and variants
Technic	Pentascale and triad patterns and variants to be practiced daily in set keys with a metronome	**Sightreading**	Short examples, with skills checklist
Prepared Sightreading	Questions and a short musical excerpt	**Aural Skills-Rhythmic**	Beat Clap-Along Echo Clap
Aural Skills-Rhythmic	Clapping (non-metrical), metrical patterns, writing and memorization	**Aural Skills-Pitch**	High-Low Identification Echo-Sing Melody Completion
Aural Skills-Pitch	Shape and pattern recognition, pitch matching, singing		

How much time should you spend on basic skills? The best choice, of course, is to spend a moderate amount of time daily on technic, sightreading and ear training. But even a smaller amount of time each day, every day is better than spending a lot of time on one day after several days of non-practice.

The Open Plan System

The Open Plan organization of the *American Popular Piano Skills* books encourages skill acquisition at each student's natural pace. Review the chart on the left to help understand how it works.

How should you schedule assignments of Prep Skills? Progress will vary depending on each student's needs and practice timetable.

- **Faster moving students** can do one module per week.
- **Many students** will do two or three skill areas within a module per week. Teachers often assign Technic for daily practice, at increasing metronome speeds.
- **Students with less practice time** often do just one skill area per week.

Areas that need extra work may, of course, be repeated as necessary.

Some Basic Tips

Clapping Traditional clapping only shows the starting-place of a note, not its duration. I ask students to "shake" (a quick up-down motion with clasped hands) for each extra beat. A whole note, for example, would be clap-shake-shake-shake.

Singing Many students have never experienced singing—at all! It will take some time and patience for them to find their voices. I play a note on the piano, ask students to pretend their voice is a butterfly, and to have the butterfly fly up and down (sing up and down) until it finds the note. Most students can sing middle C and neighboring notes.

Aural Skills – Pitch
Here is an example of a successfully completed question 1. Draw lines connecting the notes to visually reinforce the shape. Then write in each correct interval.

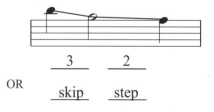

OR

3	2
skip	step

Mix Do you have to do all activities for every section? It's up to you. You'll make the right decision based on available time, skill level and long-term goals. Remember, the most important factor in improving fundamentals is: **work on them — and do it often!!**